Men-at-Arms • 209

The War in Cambodia 1970–75

K Conboy & K Bowra • Illustrated by M Chappell

Series editor Martin Windrow

First published in Great Britain in 1989 by Osprey Publishing,
Midland House, West Way, Botley, Oxford OX2 0PH, UK
43-01 21st Street, Suite 220B, Long Island City, NY 11101, USA
Email: info@ospreypublishing.com

Osprey Publishing is part of the Osprey Group.

Transferred to digital print on demand 2007

First published 1989
2nd impression 2001

Printed and bound by Cadmus Communications, USA

A CIP catalogue record for this book is available from the British Library

ISBN: 978 0 85045 851 0

Index by Margaret Vaudrey

The Woodland Trust
Osprey Publishing is supporting the Woodland Trust, the UK's leading woodland
conservation charity, by funding the dedication of trees.

www.ospreypublishing.com

The Course of the War

In 1953 the French granted Cambodia full independence, allowing the youthful Khmer King Norodom Sihanouk to lead the first post-French colonial sovereign government in Indochina. For ten years Sihanouk (who abdicated the throne in 1955, but retained political leadership) attempted to follow a non-aligned foreign policy, steering Cambodia along a neutralist tightrope which would keep it from being dragged into the wars in neighbouring Laos and South Vietnam. In November 1963, however, Sihanouk stated that US economic and military aid would be renounced as of January 1964. A break in diplomatic relations followed, and Cambodia's foreign policy began to lean toward the left.

From 1964 until 1966 Sihanouk showed increasing accommodation toward the North Vietnamese and Viet Cong. In March 1965, he hosted the Indochinese People's Conference, attended by Pathet Lao and Viet Cong representatives, which concluded with a general condemnation of the US presence in South-East Asia. At the same time, Chinese, Soviet, and Czechoslovakian military aid began to filter into the country. The Chinese even promised to support a 49,000-man *Forces Armées Royales Khmere*—FARK—19,000 more troops than the country then boasted.

Three years after his move to the left, the mercurial Sihanouk shifted again. A new conservative National Assembly took office, prompting an alarmed Cambodian Communist Party to launch its first major attacks against government outposts in April 1967. Sihanouk sent paratroopers to quell the revolt, but the surviving Communists—now armed with stolen weapons—were able to escape into the countryside to being organising a wider insurgency. This became the beginning of what Sihanouk called the *Khmer Rouge* (Red Cambodian) guerrilla forces.

Five months later, after a crisis in relations with

China, Sihanouk agreed to greater North Vietnamese use of the Cambodian port of Sihanoukville for shipping supplies to base areas along the South Vietnamese border. (It was later determined that, at its peak, Sihanoukville handled 80 per cent of North Vietnamese supplies destined for the war in South Vietnam.) At the same time he publicly announced that the Vietnamese presence on Cambodian territory was not sanctioned by the Phnom Penh government. He also hinted that he would not be opposed to US forces entering Cambodia in 'hot pusuit' of Communist units. This

A FARK captain from the 1ᵉʳ *Bataillon de Parachutistes*, 1960. He wears French parachute wings on a French 1951 camouflaged jump-smock, and a US helmet liner. The belt buckle bears the royal coat of arms in gold. Ceremonial swords were presented to graduating members of the *Ecole Militaire Khmere*.

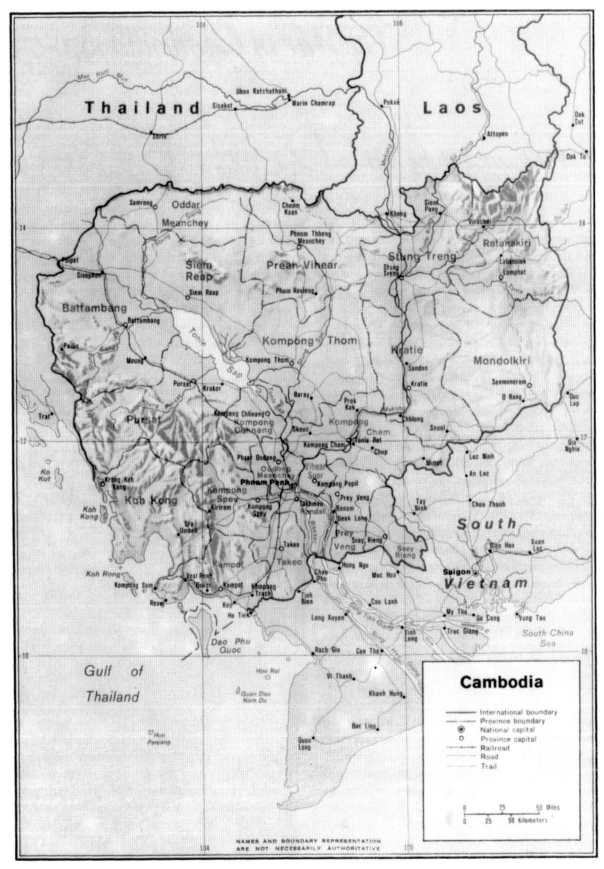

Cambodia

— International boundary
--- Province boundary
⊛ National capital
○ Province capital
Railroad
Road
Trail

0   25   50 Miles
0   25   50 Kilometers

right of pursuit, with Sihanouk's approval, was later extended to B-52 strikes on North Vietnamese Army (NVA) base areas.

In his attempt to appease all sides while maintaining a façade of neutrality, Sihanouk was alienating important segments of the country. The FARK, in particular, were frustrated by their inability to counter the extensive Vietnamese presence in the eastern border region. They were also unimpressed with the small amounts of Communist aid delivered since US military assistance was cut in 1964.

1970

With domestic opposition in Phnom Penh growing increasingly vocal, Sihanouk left in early 1970 for a state visit to China and the Soviet Union. During his absence the National Assembly unanimously voted him out of office on 18 March 1970. He was replaced by the commander of the FARK, Gen. Lon Nol, who immediately began to set a new course for the country. The Kingdom of Cambodia became a pro-Western Republic, the Communist Vietnamese were ordered to leave Cambodian territory, and an open appeal was made to the West for assistance in bolstering the newly rechristened *Forces Armées Nationales Khmere*—(FANK).

Within days of the change in government, the FANK went into action against the NVA. Massing elements of its airborne, armour, and artillery forces, the FANK drove toward the town of Baret, 90 miles south-east of Phnom Penh. Fighting raged for a week, after which the outnumbered and outclassed FANK were forced to withdraw from the border area. At the same time, the Army of the Republic of Vietnam (ARVN) and US forces launched a full-scale assault on NVA sanctuaries in Cambodia. The ARVN went on to conduct several major ground operations against NVA concentrations in Cambodia over the following years.

Brig.Gen. Fanmoung (right: note gold star on black chest tab, and no less than seven pens in sleeve pocket), commander of the First Military Region in November 1970, inspects a FANK squad. Uniforms are basically olive drab, with light OD or khaki headgear; the berets are khaki (sergeant at left, with gold chest chevrons and M3 'grease-gun') or, in the general's case, very light OD with a tan leather rim. (Courtesy Col. Harry Amos)

A Khmer Krom platoon, newly arrived from South Vietnam with their US-style jungle fatigues and M16s, parade at Tonle Bet in November 1970. Blue-over-yellow or blue-over-white tabs are worn slanting on the left breast as unit identification; the man at front right has blue and yellow tassels on his M16; the NCO at front, second from right, wears one gold over two red/yellow mixed chevrons. (Courtesy Col. Harry Amos)

Soon after the FANK suffered its first setbacks at the hands of the NVA, the United States began a military aid programme to the Khmer Republic. On 22 April 1970, thousands of captured Communist rifles were sent to Phnom Penh. In May the US also assembled 2,000 Khmer Krom soldiers and airlifted them to Cambodia. (The Khmer Krom, a term used to designate ethnic Khmer living in South Vietnam, had fought for years in units under the control of the US Army Special Forces.) By the end of 1970 eight Khmer Krom battalions were deployed in Cambodia.

Other Free World forces offered assistance to the Khmer Republic, including the Republic of China, South Korea, Indonesia, and Thailand. In July 1970 2,000 FANK soldiers went for 16 weeks of military training in Thailand. The Thais also agreed to train 2,500 ethnic Khmer volunteers living in Thailand; this programme was later halted because of funding problems.

With assistance from the USA, Phnom Penh began to expand and reorganise the FANK. In July—in the midst of reorganising—the FANK had its first taste of heavy fighting. Reacting to a lull in enemy activity, the FANK attempted to use the opportunity to raise the morale of its troops by retaking large expanses of rich rice-growing areas not under government control. The plan, launched in late August, was named Operation 'Chenla'. Ten infantry battalions supported by armour and artillery, converged on Route 6 to sweep away the enemy forces along the highway and recapture the rice paddies around Kompong Thom. Although 15 miles of Route 6 were opened for a short time, the NVA 9th Division hit back hard and threw the FANK on to the defensive for most of the operation. Only some of 'Chenla's' objectives were achieved, and at the expense of sacrificing some of the best Khmer Krom battalions.

1971

As 'Chenla' was drawing to a close, the year 1971 opened with a dramatic demonstration of a new Communist strategy designed to keep the Republic off balance by striking deep into the heart of government population centres. On the night of 21

January 1971 100 Communist Vietnamese commandos mounted a sapper attack on Pochentong Airbase outside Phnom Penh. Almost the entire Khmer Air Force was destroyed on the ground. Coinciding with this attack, other Communist units hit the capital's naval base and other villages in the vicinity of Phnom Penh. The strikes had the desired effect of forcing the FANK to recall some of the 'Chenla' task force to reinforce the capital. From that time forward the FANK General Headquarters focused on consolidating its hold over the major population centres, leaving the countryside open to Khmer Rouge recruiting drives.

Following the Pochentong attack President Lon Nol suffered a stroke. When he returned to office in April 1971 preparations were made for a second, more ambitious offensive to open all of Route 6 and to secure the road between Kompong Cham and the isolated garrison at Kompong Thom. The operation, codenamed 'Chenla Two', relied heavily on air power to soften up an estimated two NVA divisions in the region. 'Chenla Two' was launched on 20 August 1971, catching the NVA by surprise and succeeding in opening the entire highway in just over two weeks. Consolidation efforts continued until 25 October, when 'Chenla Two' was officially concluded. Celebrations had hardly started when the 9th NVA Division, reinforced by the 205th and 207th Regional Regiments, cut off and systematically eliminated the FANK task force. By early December, ten government battalions plus another ten battalions-worth of equipment had been lost.

1972

The FANK, now with many of its finest units destroyed, launched two small operations at the beginning of 1972. The first, Operation 'Angkor Chey', was an attempt to clear enemy forces from the revered Angkor Wat temple complex. The second, Operation 'Prek Ta', was planned in conjunction with ARVN units south of Route 1. Neither initiative succeeded, and the FANK was forced to pull back to Phnom Penh once again.

In March 1972 a lull in Communist activity ended when the enemy began heavy attacks on Prey Veng City and Neak Luong. ARVN troops crossed the border to engage the NVA 1st Division in the region, confronting the North Vietnamese in three major ground assaults around Kompong

Trach. At the same time, Khmer insurgents hit the capital with a devastating rocket attack: 200 rounds of 122mm rocket and 75mm recoilless rifle fire struck, killing over a hundred people. A second round of shelling and sapper attacks hit Phnom Penh in May, killing 28 people inside the city. In response, the FANK launched several sweeps around the capital, temporarily silencing the elusive rocket teams.

Not allowing the FANK to pin them down, the Khmer Communists shifted their attack and began a sabotage campaign against shipping along the Mekong. On 23 March two cargo vessels were hit by sappers near Phnom Penh. That same week, floating mines destroyed two POL barges. Government garrisons along the Mekong River were also hit. Reacting to the newest threat, the FANK combined with the ARVN in July to clear the enemy from the Mekong corridor. Strong NVA forces in the region intervened, using tanks and SAM-7 anti-aircraft missiles for the first time in Cambodia. With heavy air support, the combined task force captured the town of Kompong Trabeck in August. The garrison was turned over to the FANK, only to be lost permanently in September after renewed fighting.

For the remainder of 1972 the Communist forces

A FANK reconnaissance platoon parades in South Vietnam after completing advanced training; their tiger-striped jungle hats distinguish them from ordinary infantry trainees.

Psychological warfare teams erected billboards depicting the Vietnamese enemy faced by Cambodia.

harassed government lines of communication, impeding the flow of supplies to Phnom Penh and causing a minor rice riot in the capital. Supply traffic along the Mekong River, the Republic's major lifeline, was also attacked by Communist frogmen.

1973
In January 1973 the insurgents ignored a Republican ceasefire, launching their dry season offensive during the same month. By March the situation was growing critical as enemy attacks struck north of Phnom Penh and along the Mekong corridor. After six months the enemy offensive shifted to a more direct assault on Phnom Penh. The government reacted with massive air support, inflicting tremendous casualties on the Communist forces during August.

As the fighting around Phnom Penh began to subside, a second Communist front was opened against the provincial capital of Kompong Cham. Insurgents stormed Kompong Cham in August and occupied half of the city, capturing the hospital and brutally massacring its patients. At the same time, US air power was withdrawn from Cambodia on 15 August, throwing the defence of Kompong Cham completely into the hands of the Cambodian armed forces. By means of a naval armada, reinforcements from the infantry, marines, paratroopers, and Special Forces were lifted to government positions across the Mekong from the besieged city. On 10 September an amphibious assault was made into the Communist-held quarter of Kompong Cham, overwhelming the insurgents and regaining full control of the city after a month of fighting.

1974
Although the FANK had to commit over four brigades to the operation, the victory at Kompong Cham was savoured by the government. It gave them new confidence, and generally boosted morale in an army which had not seen a major victory in years. Their high spirits lasted until January 1974, when the Communists opened their latest dry season offensive with an attack on Phnom Penh. An estimated two enemy regiments moved within five kilometres north-west of the capital, only to lose 300 men when elements of the FANK 1st Division responded effectively.

After the north-western threat was pushed back, Communist pressure moved to the south-west as an insurgent thrust broke through the lines of the FANK 3rd Division. Inexperienced units withdrew in disorder, allowing the Communists to advance unopposed. Reinforcements from neighbouring units were rushed in on 20 January, stabilising the situation by the end of the month.

In an attempt to break Communist momentum, the FANK moved on to the offensive in February. Striking north-west and south of the capital, the Republican forces succeeded in driving the insurgents back. The Communists reacted by bringing in captured 105mm artillery pieces and shelling Phnom Penh from a distance, killing over 200 civilians on 11 February alone. As the FANK moved against the artillery positions the Communists shifted their attack yet again, this time by increasing the number of strikes against Mekong supply convoys.

By the following month the insurgents had left the Phnom Penh region and were concentrating their forces against two provincial capitals, Oudong and Kampot. In Kampot the government's position had deteriorated rapidly when 300 troops from the isolated garrison deserted. Before the insurgents could capitalise on the opportunity, however, two FANK brigades were rushed in, bolstering the town's defences and inflicting close to 300 enemy casualties. In April Kampot once again came under attack, requiring an airmobile rein-

forcement of two battalions. By 9 April over 4,000
FANK defenders occupied the besieged garrison,
sustaining over 400 killed while inflicting an
estimated 2,300 enemy casualties during the period
March–May 1974.

The situation at Oudong was more serious. On 2
March a Communist assault pushed 700 government troops and 1,500 civilians into a small enclave
south-east of Oudong. A FANK task force was
ferried up the Tonle Sap to link up with the
defenders, but insurgent forces were waiting for
them with 75mm recoilless rifles and B-40 rockets.
Twenty-five troops were killed at debarkation and
one UH-1H helicopter was shot down. While the
remainder of the task force was linking up with the
surviving members of the garrison, the civilian
population swelled to an unmanageable 4,000
refugees inside the tiny perimeter. The Communists
hit with several ground assaults and overran the
camp. Only 650 people broke through to friendly
lines; the remainder were presumed dead. A
susequent FANK drive succeeded in recapturing
the burned-out town.

The 1974 wet season began in June with a period
of lessened military activity. As the FANK
attempted to regain lost ground around the capital,
it made the belated discovery that its superior
tactical manoeuvrability made the slower and
increasingly conventional insurgent forces vulner-
able to being 'whip-sawed'. Several government
operations were launched, each handing the
Communists a tactical setback. One notable
operation conducted during this time was the relief

Cannibalised T-37 light ground-attack aircraft edge the
runway at Pochentong Airbase, still bearing ARK markings.

of the surrounded garrison at Kompong Seila,
suffering under a record eight-month siege. Radio
reports from the garrison indicated that the civilian
population were starving and, in some cases,
resorting to cannibalism. Complicating matters, the
garrison had deviated from standard FANK
communications procedures, raising fears that
Kompong Seila might be a Communist trap. After
two unsuccessful attempts, a heliborne Special
Forces team was flown in at first light. After
verification of the loyalty of the garrison, resupply
operations were sanctioned, alleviating the star-
vation and allowing Kompong Seila to hold out
successfully against further Communist pressure.

Government successes continued throughout the
rest of the year. South of Phnom Penh, a concerted
effort was made during September to clear the
banks of the Bassac River using two infantry task
forces with M113 APC support. Heavy fighting
flared along the river until December, with heavy
casualties on both sides. In a final drive, the M113
APC squadrons from four FANK divisions were
combined for a sweep of the west bank of the Bassac,
killing 63 enemy soldiers before the operation closed
on 31 December.

1975
The year 1975 opened with a new, determined
Communist offensive. Fighting was concentrated
along the Mekong corridor and within 15
kilometres of Phnom Penh. The four FANK

infantry divisions gathered around the captial, while the 1st Parachute Brigade was sent to hold the territory across the Mekong to the east. Air force and naval assets were also pulled back around the capital. Despite their best efforts, the Republican forces were unable to stop the Communist advance. The situation worsened on 1 April when the commander of the Neak Luong garrison, the last major government post on the Upper Mekong, called for air strikes on his own crumbling position. With the loss of Neak Luong the government's Mekong lifeline was cut. An air bridge to Phnom Penh was created, only to be halted on 14 April when Pochentong Airbase came under heavy rocket attack. With no further avenues for resupply—and a request for additional aid dropped by President Ford on 15 April—the Cambodian armed forces dug into their final ammunition reserves.

On 17 April, the refugee-swollen city of Phnom Penh grew silent: the Republican government had surrendered, and the Communist insurgents were pouring into the capital. The war was over; but for the people of Cambodia, the nightmare had just begun.

U.S. Military Assistance

When the Khmer Republic entered the war in South-East Asia, anti-war sentiment in the United States was reaching a peak. As a result, the Cooper-Church Amendment, proposed in April 1970 and set to go into effect by 1971, prevented US military personnel from advising Khmer units in Cambodia. Instead, a number of peripheral organisations were quickly assembled to handle assistance to Cambodia without violating the rules laid down by the US Congress. In South Vietnam, the US Army-Vietnam Individual Training Group, jointly established by USARV and MACV on 24 February 1971, was tasked with training battalion-sized FANK units. UITG Headquarters was established at Bien Hoa, utilising the former Co. A Headquarters of the US Army 5th Special Forces

A 'Cedar Walk' team assembles at Long Thanh, South Vietnam, before an operation into Cambodia.

Group. Training camps were set up at Long Hai, Chi Lang, Phuc Tuy, and Dong Ba Thin, with a US Army Special Forces A Detachment at each location. The majority of US personnel in UITG were Special Forces-qualified, though not assigned to a Special Forces Group. Other UITG personnel included members of the US Marine Corps, Australian Advisory Training Team, and New Zealand Special Air Service. Additional US Army Special Forces teams from the 1st Special Forces Group in Okinawa supplemented the UITG programme on a temporary duty basis.

UITG instruction cycles for FANK battalions lasted 13 weeks and included individual weapons training, squad-, platoon-, company-, and battalion-level training. The programme was very rigid, and concluded with company and battalion field operations against NVA/VC in areas close to the training camp. Enemy contact became more frequent and resulted in some large clashes, to include two FANK battalions against the 333rd NVA Main Force Regiment in April 1972.

Following the completion of a training cycle, the FANK battalions were issued ammunition and returned to Phnom Penh aboard C-130 aircraft. On 15 May 1972 UITG was redesignated the FANK Training Command, Army Advisory Group, Vietnam. FTC remained active until 30 November 1972. A total of 85 Cambodian battalions were trained, including basic light infantry, airborne, marine, and Khmer Special Forces cadres.

To co-ordinate material deliveries to the FANK, a Special Support Group was established in MACV J-4 during May 1970. Various staff sections of MACV provided individuals and groups to study the Cambodian situation, survey requirements, and participate in plans to assist the Khmer Republic in mobilising and equipping its armed forces. One of their first acts was to ship large quantities of captured Communist and outdated US weapons to Phnom Penh. In addition, ethnic Khmer units previously under the control of the US Army Special Forces in South Vietnam, as well as a re-equipped Khmer Brigade previously evacuated to South Vietnam, were rushed to Cambodia. Other forms of support, ranging from aerial resupply

A FANK armoured crew stand behind an M113 equipped with a 106mm recoilless rifle and a .50 cal. MG turret. The man at left wears a cloth Armoured Brigade patch over his right breast pocket; second left has a silver metal version.

A FANK lieutenant-colonel—wearing US jungle fatigues, khaki beret, and ranking on a black chest tab—talks with the commander of the MEDTC.

delivery of equipment; and observe the utilisation of US material and Cambodian personnel trained by the US and third countries. In this last capacity MEDTC personnel often followed Cambodian units into combat, stretching—at times—the restraints of the Cooper-Church Amendment. No members of the MEDTC were killed in Cambodia, however.

In April 1975 MEDTC continued to arrange and control aerial resupply missions into Phnom Penh from its rear base in Thailand. On 12 April its remaining members inside Cambodia were evacuated with the rest of the US Mission. Five days later, the Khmer Republic fell and the MEDTC mission was terminated.

A third US military group which actively assisted the Cambodian Armed Forces was the US Army 46th Special Forces Company headquartered at Lopburi, Thailand. Detachment A-42 from the 46th Co. was used during 1971–72 in Operation 'Freedom Runner', the training programme for the Khmer Special Forces. Detachment A-41 (Ranger) was used later to conduct advanced ranger courses for selected members of the Khmer Special Forces, sometimes following the Cambodian students on training forays into north-western Cambodia.

The Cambodian Armed Forces

The Cambodian Army
On 20 November 1946 a French-Khmer military agreement was signed, signalling official French recognition of the *Forces Armées Royales Khmere*. Three days later the first FARK battalion was formed from elements of the Khmer National Guard and the Cambodian Rifle Regiment of the French Union Army. Still under French command, the FARK saw its first combat against the Viet Minh in 1947. Small operations continued over the next three years, with the FARK gradually assuming responsibility for the defence of Battambang and Kompong Thom Province.

In 1953 the FARK began to participate in demonstrations for complete Cambodian independence. By October, with hundreds of Khmer soldiers having deserted French-led units, the French High Command agreed to transfer re-

shipments to close air support, were provided throughout 1970. By the end of the year, however, it became apparent that a single group was needed to administer support for Cambodia. In December 1970 an MACV study group advocated the establishment of a Military Equipment Delivery Team, Cambodia.

The MEDTC was activated in Phnom Penh on 31 January 1971. It was originally authorised at 16 personnel in Cambodia and 44 in Saigon. As the tempo of military shipments increased, however, the MEDTC contingent in Cambodia could not keep abreast of determining requests to support the FANK's mobilisation, much less execute even minimally the statutory requirements for monitoring and executing a Military Assistance Programme. Eventually, 50 MEDTC members were allowed to enter Cambodia provided the majority were fluent in French. By December 1971 the number had again been raised to 62.

The three fold purpose of the MEDTC was to determine the needs of the FANK; arrange for the sponsibility for Cambodian national security to the FARK. France, however, maintained the right to station units in north-eastern Cambodia to guard its communications links.

In late March 1954, with most French resources focused on the siege of Dien Bien Phu in Tonkin, the fully independent FARK was forced to conduct its first solo operation when the Viet Minh 436/101 Battalion crossed from southern Laos into north-eastern Cambodia and overran a company of the French-led *9' Bataillon d'Infanterie*. The insurgents pushed south until May, seizing Prek Te and securing control over the middle section of the Mekong. The FARK sent the *1" Bataillon de Parachutistes Khmere* to lead the counter-attack, recapturing the lost positions by July and successfully completing the first Khmer-led operation.

After the Geneva Convention was signed in 1954 the final transfer of remaining Khmer units in the French Union Army was completed, raising FARK strength to 45,000 men. By the end of the following year, however, FARK manpower had been cut back to 36,000. As Cambodia maintained the façade of a neutral foreign policy, the FARK shifted its focus to civic action programmes. When US military aid was cut in 1954 the FARK regressed into a poorly equipped, under-strength force of 18,000 men.

The FARK's poor state of readiness became apparent in the mid-1960s when the joint threat from Khmer Communist insurgents and right wing Khmer Serei forces presented the first major challenges to the Cambodian government since the First Indochina War. An even bigger threat was posed by the NVA/VC forces in eastern Cambodia, the target of a restrained FARK sweeping operation in November 1969. Against these, the FARK fielded in January 1970 some 53 battalions and 11 regional companies. Slightly over half of the battalions were designated *Bataillons d'Infanterie*; the remainder were *Bataillons de Chasseurs*, or light infantry battalions. Three formations—the paratroopers, Phnom Penh Garrison, and Royal Guard—were organised into half-brigades. Anti-aircraft, artillery, engineer, and transport groups also formed half-brigades, while armoured units were split into an independent battalion at Kompong Cham and a regiment at Sre Khlong. All

A US Defence Attaché receives a medal from President Lon Nol and Chief of Staff Sak Sutsakhan. Note General Headquarters combined service patch on Gen. Sak's shoulder; Lon Nol wears a metal version of this insignia on his right breast. (Courtesy Col. Harry Amos)

other battalions acted independently while assigned either to the General Reserve or Military Regions.

By March 1970 the confrontation between head of state Norodom Sihanouk and the supporters of Gen. Lon Nol gave rise to rumours of an impending coup against Sihanouk. Anti-Communist Khmer Serei rebel forces in contact with disgruntled senior members of the FARK were aware of this situation, and had infiltrated close to the capital. Three Khmer Serei battalions from the Dongrek Mountains, one ethnic Khmer battalion from the ARVN 25th Division, and Khmer Krom elements from the Tien Bien 'Mike Force' camp in South Vietnam were near the outskirts of Phnom Penh when Gen. Lon Nol assumed power on 17 March.

Immediately following the ousting of Sihanouk, the rechristened *Forces Armées Nationales Khmere* faced opposition from vastly superior NVA forces. Under strength and poorly equipped, the army mounted an immediate recruitment drive. By June,

One of two AC-47 gunships on the eve of its delivery to the Khmer Republic, June 1971. A double and a single .50 cal. MG mount can be seen in the windows immediately forward of the door. (Courtesy Doug Blair)

18 General Reserve infantry brigades had been created; however, only 12 brigades were properly manned, the rest remaining only on paper.

Several programmes were quickly implemented to help the FANK reach its July 1970 authorised troop strength of 206,000 men. Khmer Serei forces previously operating in the Dongrek Mountains were retrained in Thailand and used as the core of a Special Brigade in Siem Reap. This brigade was later expanded into the highly-rated 9th Brigade Group. Eight Khmer Krom battalions from the South Vietnamese irregular forces were also sent to Phnom Penh. In addition, the 1st FANK Shock Brigade, evacuated to South Vietnam after its garrison in Ratanakiri province fell, was re-equipped and airlifted back to Cambodia. A more regimented FANK training programme began in 1971 in South Vietnam.

As it expanded rapidly the FANK became divided into a confusing array of French and US combat organisations. The largest was the brigade group, normally composed of two brigades. Other formations included half-brigades, autonomous regiments, independent brigades, groups, and territorial battalions. In addition, a paramilitary Gendarmerie was formed to extend the government presence across the countryside. In early 1972 the FANK continued to employ the brigade group as its largest combat organisation. Of the 15 brigade groups fielded in January 1972, however, only three were rated as being militarily effective; three were still in South Vietnam training; and nine were considered to be only marginally reliable. In April 1972 the FANK subdivided its forces further by splitting its General Reserve into three groups: *Forces A* were attached to a military zone for operations; *Forces B*, numbering five brigades, were designated as the General Staff Reserve; *Forces C*, totalling two airborne battalions, were Lon Nol's reserve.

During its expansion the FANK had continued to rely heavily on a steady flow of Khmer Krom recruits from South Vietnam. Traditionally aggressive, the Khmer Krom brought with them years of combat experience gained while fighting in South Vietnam. In February 1972 some 13 infantry brigades, and the Khmer Special Forces, had high percentages of Khmer Krom troops. Due to extensive casualties during Operations 'Chenla' and 'Chenla Two', however, the best Khmer Krom formations became diluted by non-Khmer Krom recruits; and several of the Khmer Krom units, promised six-month tours in Cambodia, grew increasingly demoralised as they were kept past their promised return dates. By March 1972 only the Khmer Krom 7th, 44th, and 51st Brigades were still rated as superior. Six months later, following the mutiny of a Khmer Krom battalion, recruiting in South Vietnam dried up and the Khmer Krom legend came to an undignified end.

Denied further Khmer Krom recruits, the FANK focused on developing its own indigenous training facilities. The Officer Candidate School, cut from a three-year to a six-month course, was moved from Phnom Penh to Longvek. Infantry training centres at Kandal and Kompong Speu were opened; construction of similar centres at Ream, Sisophon and Longvek was started. In addition, a Recondo School run by the Khmer Special Forces was opened in 1972 in Battambang.

The FANK also began expanding its village defence programmes. In July 1972 Auto-Defence units were planned for each Military Region. A more ambitious project known as the Liberation and Nation-Building Directorate was formed in November, and the first Auto-Defence pilot programme of the LNB was formed in Siem Reap during the same month. Operating closely with the LNB Directorate, a Political Warfare Directorate within the General Staff was created, along with a Political Warfare Brigade.

To streamline the mass of combat formations within the FANK, a major reorganisation was implemented in December 1972. By the following month, all brigade group headquarters, 17 regimental headquarters, 16 brigade headquarters, and 13 battalions had been dissolved. In their place, 32 brigades, 202 infantry battalions, and 405 territorial infantry companies were formed. Of these, 128 battalions were grouped into the 32 brigades. Twenty of the brigades would remain independent, with 12 being distributed among four new FANK divisions. A fifth, the understrength 9th Guards Division, was raised in April 1974 by the highly political and militarily incompetent Gen. Ith Suong.

The reorganised FANK was soon plagued with difficulties. On 28 January 1973 all South Vietnamese training concluded in conjunction with the Paris Peace Accords, depriving Cambodia of vital training assistance. Two months later the 1st Parachute Brigade, long considered one of the best FANK units, abandoned positions along the southern Mekong when their operation extended beyond the promised conclusion date. Several other brigades followed the example of the paras, leading to several unnecessary government reversals. To make matters worse, US air support—used excessively by the FANK—was revoked in August. During the same month seven Nationalist Chinese instructors on loan to the FANK Artillery School were withdrawn.

Despite these setbacks, the resilient optimism of the Cambodian soldier resulted in several brilliant performances in 1974. One of the most famous took place 14 kilometres north-east of the capital on the morning of 10 November, when an estimated two Khmer Communist regiments stormed a government outpost. The initial attack was repulsed, but two company-sized positions were overrun the following day. Rushing in the 128th Infantry Battalion, the 2nd Para Battalion, and 4th Para Battalion, the FANK garrison withstood continuous pressure for 13 days. All enemy attacks were defeated, and the two lost positions were retaken by 27 November.

By early 1975 the FANK was exhausted. Medical resources were reaching the breaking point, and foreign military aid, already preciously low, was cut in early April. On 17 April, the FANK offered its surrender to the Khmer Communist forces.

FANK troops train on the .30 cal. M1919 MG at Long Hai training base, South Vietnam, 1972.

US Army Special Forces adviser from the UITG training base at Long Hai, South Vietnam. He wears a ChiCom AK-47 chest pouch rig and an NVA bush hat. US jungle fatigues have been altered by moving the lower shirt pockets on to the upper sleeves. The weapon is a CAR-15 with modified assault sling.

Special Operations

The Khmer Republic raised several unconventional warfare units during its brief five-year existence. The largest was the Khmer Special Forces, organised in October 1971 under the command of Lt. Col. Thach Reng. Khmer Special Forces teams were sent for training at the Royal Thai Army Special Warfare Centre at Lopburi, Thailand, under Operation 'Freedom Runner'. Additional training was conducted in South Vietnam and the United States. An indigenous Special Forces training centre was also being planned shortly before the country fell.

By the time 'Freedom Runner' training was concluded in July 1973 the Khmer Special Forces had one C Detachment, three B Detachments, and 18 A Detachments. Unlike a US Army Special Forces A Team, those in the Khmer Special Forces had 15 men, the additional personnel being psychological warfare specialists.

The missions of the Khmer Special Forces ranged from strategic and tactical reconnaissance to raids, pathfinding, and providing instructors for the FANK Recondo School in Battambang. In a true special forces rôle, they also raised village militias behind enemy lines. One of their most famous missions was performed by two A Detachments during the siege at Kompong Cham in September 1973. Spearheading the government assault on the Communist-held southern quarter of the city, the teams were inserted by helicopter and used LAW rockets to neutralise an insurgent stronghold, allowing the FANK to rush in amphibious reinforcements without taking excessive casualties. Despite this success, the Special Forces remained too small to make a strategic difference. In addition, many of the regional commanders misused them as conventional shock troops, and a large portion of the Special Forces remained in Phnom Penh as a deterrent against coup attempts. By April 1975 the Special Forces were massed in Phnom Penh, and planned a breakout to the south-east toward the South Vietnamese border. They never made it, and were presumed killed in action.

Three other special operations units were under the tacit control of the Khmer Special Forces. The first consisted of repatriated elements of the MACV Studies and Observation Group 'Cedar Walk' programme. 'Cedar Walk' teams were composed of unilaterally controlled Cambodian operatives used against the NVA border sanctuaries in Cambodia. Two contingents were turned over to the Special Forces in October 1971, but political manoeuvring left them in the hands of the SEDOC, Cambodia's intelligence service. A second unit was composed of Khmer nationals trained in Laos under Project 'Copper' and stationed at Khong Island on the Mekong River. From Khong Island they were heliborne into the Communist-controlled provinces of north-eastern Cambodia, and used as recon teams along the Ho Chi Minh Trail. A third unconventional warfare unit was trained in Indonesia during 1972. Half of the returnees went to a FANK infantry brigade; the other half were used later in the war as the cadre for a Para-Commando Battalion.

In mid-1973 the Khmer Navy raised its own special warfare unit, the Cambodian SEALs. Modelled on their US counterparts, an initial group of SEAL recruits was drawn from an existing Combat Swimmer unit and sent to the United States and the Philippines for basic training. At its

FANK insignia: (top left) Khmer Republic beret flash—blue shield, white script, edge, stars, white temple motif on red canton; (top right) FANK beret badge—yellow with red outlines overall; (bottom left) General HQ—blue disc edged white, white star, yellow motif; (bottom right) 1st Armoured Squadron—light grey shield, white stars, edges, disc, red '1' and disc edge, pale blue and white tank.

peak in mid-1974 the unit fielded three teams totalling 90 commandos. Airborne training was conducted at Pochentong, while the Olympic pool in Phnom Penh was used for diving courses. The SEALs provided valuable intelligence for the MNK while acting as reconnaissance teams along the banks of the Mekong. They were also used as shock troops during the sieges at Kompong Cham and Oudong. They defended the naval base opposite Phnom Penh until the final day of the war.

Uniforms and Equipment

As early as September 1950, the US provided arms and equipment for three FARK battalions. More US equipment was being supplied indirectly through the French. After the US Military Advisory and Assistance Group was established in Phnom Penh in 1955 US equipment was channelled directly, allowing the FARK largely to standardise the use of US uniforms and equipment until 1964. After US military assistance was renounced, French, Chinese and East Bloc weapons, uniforms and equipment were received. However, graduates from the Officer Candidate School continued to receive surplus stocks of coveted American materials.

The basic FARK work uniform was the khaki shirt and pants. Shorts and short-sleeved shirts were worn as the weather dictated. Army officers were given a white dress uniform with gold buttons depicting the symbol of the kingdom. In the field, Cambodian soldiers engaged in civic action programmes wore a combination of US and French fatigue clothing. Only the élite Airborne Half-Brigade wore camouflage: this included French camouflage uniforms for paratroop officers and an indigenous spotted camouflage pattern for NCOs.

After March 1970 the FANK quickly adopted both US jungle fatigues and OG 107 uniforms. Camouflage tiger-stripe uniforms from Thailand and South Vietnam were worn by some units; Indigenous tiger-stripes and leaf-pattern camouflage were also developed. The paratroopers continued to wear French-style camouflage and the indigenous spotted uniform; shortages led to officers and NCOs using both patterns indiscriminately

after 1973. The FANK dress uniform consisted of an olive green jacket and slacks with a white shirt and black tie.

FARK headgear was diverse. The most common item was a light khaki beret worn French style. A khaki peaked cap was issued to officers. Both were worn with a metal cap device bearing the royal crest, a Cambodian throne with two temple lions. Paratroopers were issued a red beret. In the field French bush hats, US patrol caps, and M1 steel helmets were worn. During the Republic khaki, camouflage, and dark green berets were issued in addition to US patrol caps and M1 steel helmets.

Footwear for the FARK initially came from both US and French sources; US jungle and black leather boots were standardised during the Republic. Belts were of black leather or canvas with a silver or gold metal buckle. After 1970, buckles sometimes bore the combined service insignia of the FANK General Staff.

Following several attacks on government airbases, the KAF trained security battalions to patrol major facilities. These troops carry an assortment of M1 Garands, M16s and an AK-47. Note 'Air Force' title above national flag shoulder patch; and cloth KAF wing insignia worn by all KAF personnel, above left breast pockets.

Nametapes were commonly worn during the Republic in both subdued cloth and plastic versions. They were usually worn over the right chest pocket, although officers were occasionally seen with nameplates on the left side. FARK rank insignia closely followed the French pattern. Shoulder boards were worn by officers, with rank similar to the French system except that generals wore stars above gold laurel-like leaf embroidery on the outer edge. Gold and silver bands were worn by other officer ranks. FARK shoulder boards were very dark blue or black for the army; paratroopers wore light green; and medics wore maroon boards. Officers also wore rank on chest tabs or shoulder loops. A royal crown design was incorporated on the inner end of shoulder boards. In the FANK the basic rank system was retained except for the royal crown being eliminated from the shoulder boards; the various coloured shoulder boards were also eliminated, being replaced by a standard black. In addition, black shoulder loops and collar rank insignia were in use by 1972.

Collar branch insignia were popularised in the FARK, in both brass and enamelled forms. Branch insignia were less frequently worn in the FANK. In 1972 yellow branch insignia embroidered on green tabs were seen worn over the right pocket. Armoured branch insignia in metal and silk woven forms were also worn above the right pocket.

Because of resistance by the royal government, the use of unit insignia was discouraged in the FARK. Those that were allowed to wear unit crests and insignia, such as the paratroopers, wore them French-style on the left breast or on the upper left sleeve. Metal and cloth parachutist wings were displayed above the right breast pocket. In the FANK unit insignia became more common, being worn on the right chest, left chest, or left shoulder. Paratroopers occasionally wore either FANK national insignia or metal wings on their berets.

The Cambodian Air Force

The *Aviation Royale Khmere* was officially founded in April 1955 with a mixed inventory of six light transports, four trainers, and 22 light aircraft suitable for conversion to the ground attack rôle. Commanded by Prince Sihanouk's personal physician, the ARK was known sarcastically as the Royal Flying Club. In accordance with Cambodia's

Like most South-East Asian armies, FANK personnel often took their families with them on active service. This soldier relaxes in a traditional red and white male *sarong*.

neutralist foreign policy, few combat missions were flown. There was one exception in March 1964, when two Cambodian T-28 fighters penetrated over two miles into South Vietnam and shot down an L-19 light aircraft in retaliation for a South Vietnamese strike into Cambodia.

After 1964 Cambodia turned to China and the Eastern Bloc for military aircraft. Five Soviet MiG-17 fighters were delivered on 9 April 1967. Student pilots were also sent to the Soviet Union for training. Not to be outdone, the Chinese sent 11 planes to Phnom Penh in January 1968.

In 1968 the ARK received its first sustained combat experience when it was tasked with bombing Khmer Rouge forces in Battambang Province; but it was not until the change of government in March 1970 that the air force, whose name had changed to the Khmer Air Force, was thrown into heavy combat. KAF MiG jets bombed and strafed NVA concentrations along the eastern border, while T-28s were used on combat sorties near Kompong Cham and north of the capital. During this period, Thai T-28s also began to provide air support in the west.

An initial expansion of the KAF was accom-

Khmer Special Forces captain at Pochentong Airbase, 1973. He wears Cambodian tiger-stripe camouflage uniform, a green beret pulled left with the Khmer Special Forces flash, three gold rank bars on black shoulder strap slides, and—over his right pocket—metal US parachutist wings, presented during 'Freedom Runner' training at Lopburi, Thailand. (Courtesy Thach Saren)

influx of US aircraft. Among the most effective additions were two AC-47 gunships armed with .50 cal. machine guns, turned over to Cambodia in mid-1971. By the end of 1971 the KAF numbered 16 T-28s, 24 0-1D light aircraft, 19 C-47 transports, nine T-41 trainers, 11 UH-1H helicopters, 16 U-1A liaison aircraft, and three AC-47 gunships.

In 1972 KAF expansion slowed slightly as organisational difficulties were encountered. Training remained a key problem: despite the loan of instructor pilots from Nationalist China, insufficient numbers of Cambodian pilots were available. KAF morale was also suffering, due mainly to 14 T-28 crashes being recorded in a twelve-month period. Confidence in the T-28 eroded, even though eight of the crashes were due to pilot error. In addition, because of plentiful US air support, the KAF was relegated to a minor rôle only.

In March of the following year the KAF suffered a further setback when a pro-Sihanouk T-28 pilot bombed the presidential palace, killing 43 people. A new KAF commander was appointed, who immediately began to enforce new programmes to improve the KAF before US air power was withdrawn on 15 August. The most important of these plans was the establishment of a KAF Direct Air Support Centre. Located in the FANK Combined Operations Centre, the DSOC was given responsibility for gathering current targeting information from US aircraft and FANK units in the field, and passing it on to the KAF. This new concept was resisted by the KAF Air Operations Co-ordination Centre, which continued to feed the KAF with pre-planned strike co-ordinates. In practice, the FANK had little faith in KAF close air support, leaving the DSOC to function primarily as a relay between the FANK Headquarters and US aircraft.

Despite an initial reluctance on the part of the ground commanders, the KAF continued to expand co-ordination with the FANK. In July the air force began providing forward air controllers to the new FANK Artillery Fire Co-ordination Centre. In addition, an Air-Ground Operations School was opened to train FANK forward air guides. During this same period the KAF broadened convoy protection operations when it took delivery of 14 Helio Au-24 mini-gunships and

plished in late 1970 under US auspices, including a delivery on 6 September of six UH-1H helicopters with temporary South Vietnamese crews. In addition, KAF students were sent to Udorn Air Base, Thailand, for T-28 training conducted by Detachment 1, 56th Special Operations Wing—a USAF training group which had been providing support to the Thai and Lao Air Forces since 1964. In January 1971, however, a North Vietnamese sapper attack on Pochentong Airbase destroyed virtually the entire KAF on the ground, including all of its MiG fighters.

Starting from scratch, the KAF received a new

six UH-1H helicopter gunships. The Au-24, used only by the KAF in a military rôle, had a 20mm cannon on a side door mount and two hardened wing points for bomb dispensers. By the following month two Au-24s and four helicopter gunships were being assigned to every convoy travelling the Mekong.

On 15 August 1973 the KAF assumed full responsibility for air support in Cambodia. Air force morale was already strained, the result of an Au-24 crash on 10 August which killed the crew and grounded the mini-gunship fleet. However, confidence improved in October following the success of Operation 'Thunderstrike', the first KAF offensive operation. For nine days, the air force struck south of Phnom Penh between Routes 2 and 3, reaching a record 70 T-28 sorties in one day. Although the 1st and 3rd FANK Divisions failed to capitilise on 'Thunderstrike', the FANK remained impressed by the KAF's performance.

Successor operations to 'Thunderstrike' were postponed in November after a second renegade T-28 pilot bombed the presidential palace and deserted. A new KAF commander, Col. Ea Chhong, was promoted and immediately began to improve the performance of the KAF. This positive reputation continued to grow in March 1974 with a successful KAF operation against the NVA Dambe Transshipment Point: some 250 trucks hidden in a plantation were destroyed in a chain reaction, a record for the Vietnam War. Resulting in part from the Dambe victory, FANK requests for KAF close air support increased. The use of forward air controllers also increased, helping the KAF conserve ordnance.

FANK, MNK and KAF representatives attend a course on air-ground delivery methods at Udorn Airbase, Thailand, 1972. The Khmer Special Forces officer (foreground, second from right) wears Thai Army and US parachutist's wings on his left breast and Cambodian basic wings on his right breast. Rear, third from left is an MNK officer wearing light grey working uniform, and his peaked cap crown is pale khaki (the stone grey is so pale it appears very similar to khaki); the MNK cap badge is embroidered in gold on black. Rear, third from right is a KAF officer wearing medium blue overseas cap and trousers, and light blue shirt. (Courtesy Capt. John Koren)

MNK insignia: (top left) MNK breast badge—yellow on white, black outlines; (top right) SEAL parachute wings—white wings and SCUBA gear, gold leaves, yellow anchor, all on black; (bottom left) *Fusiliers-Marins* shoulder insignia—dark blue shield, white stars, white temple on red canton, yellow rifles and anchor; (bottom right) SEAL shoulder insignia—red disc edged black, yellow leaves, light blue diver and anchor, black mine, yellow SCUBA tank and rope, white and black script.

KAF competence continued to grow during the opening weeks of 1975. US Defence Attaché reports written at the time judged the calibre of Cambodian pilots as fast approaching the skill level of their Thai and South Vietnamese counterparts. In an effort to further boost the KAF's capabilities, the US initiated three assistance programmes. Operation 'Rotorhead Express', started in June 1974, was a US Army programme to give a one-time repair to the KAF UH-1H fleet. Operation 'Flycatcher' was a similar USAF effort directed at the KAF T-28 fighter bombers: and in January 1975 a USAF Mobile Training Team worked with the KAF airlift wing to make it self-sufficient.

During its final months of existence the KAF exceeded all previous performances. Operating against relatively light enemy anti-aircraft defences, the KAF launched an unprecedented number of combat sorties against the insurgents massing around the capital. During a two-month period the 35 T-28D bombers in the KAF fleet logged over 1,800 missions. Using all available airframes to the limit, new delivery systems were created. Against the firmly entrenched 107mm rocket positions north of Phnom Penh, CBU-55 bomblets were dropped to great effect, killing an estimated 500 insurgents on 10 April. The smaller CBU-25 and 250 lb bombs were loaded aboard the Au-24 mini-gunship and also employed against the enemy rocket sites. In the most inventive adaption, pallets of 500 lb bombs and 25 lb fragmentation bombs were loaded aboard KAF C-123 transports and dropped by night.

Despite their best efforts, the KAF alone could not stem the tide of the advancing Communist forces. After expending virtually their entire ordnance resources, 97 aircraft escaped the country.

The ARK wore a white dress uniform and light blue work uniform. A dark blue peaked cap was worn by officers with a standard gold metal FARK badge. The KAF retained the blue peaked cap, but developed a distinctive silver metal KAF cap badge. A dark blue overseas cap was worn with the work uniform. KAF ground personnel were issued FANK-style patrol caps and fatigues. ARK rank insignia were worn on light blue shoulder boards, with a pair of stylised wings at the inner end. After March 1970 the KAF reverted to black shoulder boards or shoulder loops as worn by the FANK. ARK personnel wore gold metal wings surmounted by a royal crown on the left breast. After 1970 these were replaced with yellow wings embroidered on a blue cloth background. Both ARK and KAF pilots wore a circular gold badge on the right breast bearing *Hongsa*, a mythical Cambodian bird. Specialised support services within the KAF wore insignia on their upper left sleeve. Pilots wore squadron insignia on the upper left sleeve or right pocket.

The Cambodian Navy

The *Marine Royale Khmere* was established in 1954 to provide limited patrolling of the coast and major waterways of Cambodia. The riverine headquarters was established at Chrui Chhang War Naval Base across the Mekong from Phnom Penh; a coastal base was built at Kompong Som. Ex-French and US ships composed the bulk of its small fleet until 1964; thereafter, limited deliveries of Chinese and Eastern Bloc river and sea craft entered the MRK inventory. The Cambodians also seized a number of US riverine craft which strayed into Khmer territory, including two airboats captured from the US Army Special Forces in 1968. A Marine Corps of four *Bataillons de Fusiliers-Marins* (BFM) was maintained for static defence.

After the 1970 change of government, the rechristened *Marine Nationale Khmere* took on a more important rôle as it escorted supply convoys up the Mekong and provided logistical support for the FANK. Assisting the MNK in its new responsibilities, the South Vietnamese Navy lent extensive convoy protection and helped patrol the coastline against enemy infiltration.

By 1972 the MNK had gained enough experience to assume responsibility for convoy support operations. The KAF contributed to the effectiveness of these operations with AC-47 cover, while the South Vietnamese Air Force lent helicopter gunships to overfly convoys along the Lower Mekong. The MNK riverine forces also co-ordinated operations on the Tonle Sap in conjunction with the FANK Lake Brigade. Along the coast, the MNK continued to rely heavily on the South Vietnamese Navy to assist with coastal surveillance. Patrolling at sea became more important after South Vietnamese patrols reported in April the first attempt ·by a North Vietnemese

MNK Monitors, converted landing craft armed with 105mm guns, assemble at Chrui Chhang War Naval Base outside Phnom Penh.

vessel to infiltrate into Cambodia. The vessel was sunk, with heavy secondaries.

The MNK was challenged in early 1972 by an increase in enemy activity against Mekong shipping. After one merchant vessel was destroyed and three others damaged at the Chrui Chhang War Naval Base the MNK formed a Harbour Defence Unit. MNK defenders were further bolstered by the naval infantry, who were used for active riverbank patrolling.

Both MNK performance and enemy activity increased during the following year. In January

1973 Communist frogmen attacked merchant vessels on the Mekong; several ships were destroyed at the cost of three enemy swimmers. During the same month an enemy infiltration route was identified from Kompong Som Bay to inland supply bases. Countering these threats, the MNK maintained high morale—mainly due to sufficient rice rations, good leadership, and prompt payment of wages; and because the MNK was not highly dependent on US air power, it was not adversely affected when this support was terminated in August.

The MNK increased its efforts along the Mekong corridor in mid-1973 as the FANK began placing a higher reliance on the navy for logistical support and casualty evacuation. To handle these responsibilities the MNK increased its strength to over 13,000 men by December 1973. This included an expansion of the Marine Corps, growing from four battalions in August to nine BFMs in December. Elements of the Marines were used extensively in ground operations, including the heavy fighting at Kompong Cham in September. In addition to BFM support, the MNK ran 20 convoys between Phnom Penh and Kompong Cham under the operational order 'Castor 21', and conducted an amphibious assault by the FANK 80th Brigade into the Communist-held half of the city.

In 1974 MNK performance remained impressive. The MNK commander, Commodore Vong Sarendy, deserved much of the credit for maintaining high discipline and morale among his sailors. During that year Sarendy supervised the second major MNK amphibious operation in March when Operation 'Castor 50' delivered 30 M113 APCs, four 105mm howitzers, six trucks, and 2,740 troops to the battlefield at Oudong.

MNK strength peaked in September 1974 at 16,500 men. One-third of the total force was assigned to the Marines, whose organisation was starting to suffer from poor morale. Initially intended for static defence, the BFMs were used as intervention forces on offensive operations; ten BFMs were being used in this rôle in September,

A FANK forward air guide talks on an AN/PRC-25 radio. He wears an olive US flightsuit, and a black baseball cap from the USAF 23rd Tactical Air Support Squadron, the unit providing OV-10 forward air control coverage over Cambodia.

1: Sergeant, FARK, 1969
2: Khmer Serei guerrilla, 1969
3: Private, 1er Bn. de Parachutistes, 1971

A

1: Commando, Project 'Cedar Walk', 1971
2: Lieutenant, UITG, 1971-72
3: FANK private, Long Hai, 1972

B

1: Khmer Rouge commander, 1975
2: Khmer Rouge guerrilla, 1974
3: Khmer Rouge guerrilla, 1973

C

1: Khmer Air Force UH-1, 1973-75
2: FANK M113 APC, 1971-76

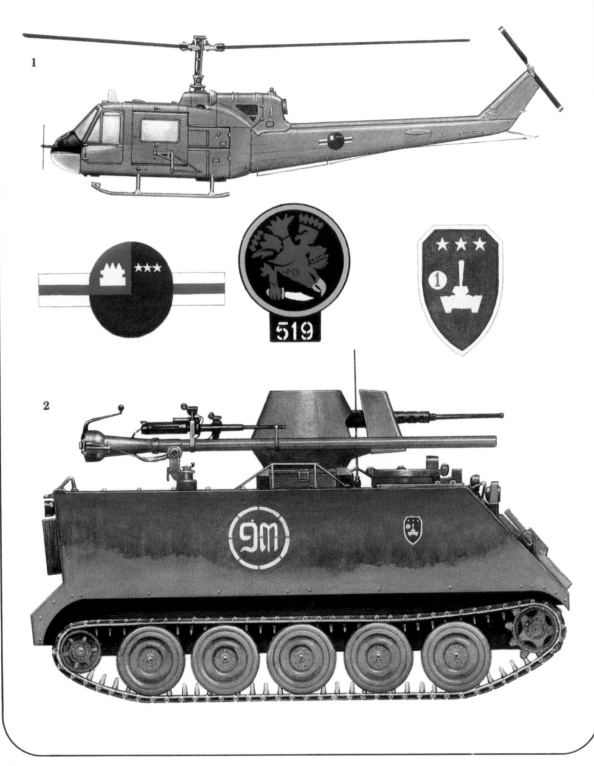

D

1: Loadmaster, Khmer Air Force, 1971
2: Captain, Khmer Air Force, 1972
3: Brig. Gen. Thach Reng, FANK SF, 1973

E

1: Sergeant, Khmer SF, 1973
2: Corporal, Bn. de Fusiliers-Marins, 1973
3: Captain, 1er Bde. Parachutiste, 1973

F

1: Captain, MEDTC, 1971-75
2: Recondo Co., 2nd FANK Division, 1974
3: Lieutenant, Bn. Para-Commando, 1975

G

1: Honour Guard, PRKAF, 1980
2: Khmer Rouge guerrilla, 1986
3: KPNLF guerrilla, 1987

H

Many women answered the FANK recruiting drives; and many, like these two, were incorporated into village militia units lightly armed with M1 carbines. Olive fatigues, khaki cap.

with the 11ᵉ BFM in training. Yet the Marines were denied hazardous duty pay comparable to that paid by the FANK, and desertions increased. The problem was never rectified.

As the 1974–1975 dry season opened, the effectiveness of the MNK was immediately curtailed by heavy enemy mining of the Mekong. Without proper minesweeping equipment the MNK remained unable to open the Mekong corridor. During the final weeks of the war the MNK riverine forces around the capital were rendered useless. Along the coast, MNK vessels lost no time in evacuating refugees to safety; as late as 9 May, three ships arrived in the Philippines with 750 passengers.

Like the rest of the Royal Armed Forces, the Royal Khmere Navy wore a white dress uniform. On other occasions a light grey work uniform was used with a matching peaked cap. Both of these uniform combinations were maintained in the MNK. A wreathed gold anchor embroidered on black was worn on the MNK peaked cap. Naval infantry wore the same fatigue uniform as the FANK. Shoulder boards in the *Marine Royale Khmere* were identical to those of the FARK, with the addition of a fouled anchor on the inner end.

During the Republic the MNK standardised the black shoulder boards or shoulder loops used in the FANK.

The MNK had several unit and qualification insignia, the former worn on the left shoulder and the latter on the right chest. An MNK pocket badge in normal and subdued forms was worn on the left breast. All BFM wore the same shoulder insignia, consisting of crossed rifles on a shield patterned after the Republican flag.

The Communist Forces

The armed Communist struggle against the Cambodian government began with the ill-fated April 1967 rebellion in Battambang Province. Although the revolt was quickly suppressed the Communists, called the Khmer Rouge by Prince Sihanouk, began to expand their insurgency. Following the March 1970 change of government the Khmer Rouge expanded their most effective village defence units into territorial forces, which soon gave way to main force elements. Prince Sihanouk, who had sought refuge in China after being deposed, contributed significantly to their growth by lending his popular support to the Communists: his leadership in the *Front Uni National du Kampuchea*, an umbrella organisation seeking the armed overthrow of the Khmer Republic, gave the anti-Republican insurgency greater legitimacy in the eyes of the Cambodian peasantry.

Conceived at the Canton Summit of April 1970, the FUNK was envisioned to include three divisions, all to be equipped by China. Imitating the Chinese experience, the insurgents would be a 'People's Army' of popular forces, territorial units, and regulars. In effect, the first FUNK units were composed of hardline Khmer Rouge, FANK defectors, and ethnic Khmer Communists aligned with the North Vietnamese. Training centres were established by the NVA in north-eastern Cambodia and Laos; a headquarters was established at Kratie, a provincial capital whose government garrison deserted soon after the change of government.

From the outset the FUNK was composed of

Command post of the 48th Brigade, one of the original Khmer Krom units, during operations on the Bassac River, 27 December 1974.

diverse and often antagonistic elements. Prominent were the hardline Khmer Rouge, who had fought Sihanouk since 1967 and advocated an extremist, agrarian, puritan form of 'primitive Communism'. Pol Pot emerged as the leader of these forces, which looked toward China as their main source of support. Also in the FUNK were a small number of intellectuals; FANK defectors; pro-Sihanoukists known as the Khmer Rumdoh; and ethnic Khmer Communists who had closely aligned themselves with the North Vietnamese. The latter two insurgent factions developed in the eastern base areas alongside the NVA, and often maintained North Vietnamese political advisors in their units. By the end of 1970 the FUNK numbered an estimated 15,000 Cambodian insurgents. Further expansion continued over the next year as the NVA

eliminated the backbone of the Republican army, allowing the FUNK quietly to build up their forces.

In 1972 the NVA decreased its force presence in Cambodia, letting the FUNK assume control in the battlefield. The FUNK by that time included some 50,000 regulars and almost 100,000 irregular supports. Throughout the year they fought a war of attrition, striking against government lines of communication and demoralising the FANK.

By January 1973, the FUNK were ready for their first full-scale solo offensive; but when they struck against Phnom Penh, air power devastated their ranks. Suffering heavy casualties, the offensive demonstrated to the FUNK leaders the need to better co-ordinate operations. In June the FUNK launched a second offensive against Phnom Penh using 75 of its 175 available battalions to converge on the capital. Although several positions were overrun south and south-west of the city, the FUNK was again devastated by ground-attack air sorties; up to 16,000 Communists perished during the offensive, with some battalions losing 60 per cent of their manpower. Significantly, most of the attackers were from the pro-Vietnamese FUNK forces, allowing the hardline Khmer Rouge to consolidate control over the more moderate Khmer Communists.

Two months later, US air support was withdrawn from Cambodia. With the Khmer Rouge in control, the FUNK muted internal dissent and prepared for its 1974 dry season offensive. Communications, command and control, and mobility were still relatively poor, resulting in unco-ordinated, piecemeal battles, and the 60,000 FUNK regulars scored no major victories against the government forces.

On 1 January 1975 the FUNK launched its 'Mekong River Offensive'. Converging on the Mekong corridor, the insurgents were able to capture the important river town of Neak Luong on 1 April. Marching north-west from the conquered corridor, the FUNK—numbering some 65,000 regulars in 12 light divisions, 40 regiments, and additional smaller units—began its final assault on the capital. Within two months a co-ordinated Communist offensive had smashed through the FANK outer perimeter and divided the Republican forces into manageable pockets of resistance. On 17

April the Khmer Rouge led the advance into the devastated capital.

FUNK uniforms and equipment reflected the various ideological backgrounds and foreign sources of support. The Khmer Rouge, which by late 1973 had become the unquestioned power behind the FUNK, wore the most spartan uniform of any Indo-Chinese insurgent group. It usually consisted of a black shirt and pants, often of local manufacture, the shirts often without pockets; pants were frequently rolled to the knee. Women conscripted into the Khmer Rouge, such as the all-female 122 Rifle Battalion, wore black pyjamas as well. Khmer Rouge armoured crews depicted in a propaganda photo next to a Chinese amphibious tank were wearing tank coveralls and helmets supplied by the NVA. (It must be noted, however, that the FUNK never used armoured vehicles in combat against the Republic.)

Other elements of the FUNK deliberately shunned black pyjamas, preferring green NVA fatigues, as worn extensively by the Khmer Rumdoh and pro-Vietnamese elements; others also wore it as a political statement in protest at the extreme, anti-Buddhist views of the Khmer Rouge. Later in the war the Khmer Rouge, too, acquired

Khmer Rouge defectors, November 1974: most wear the austere black pyjama uniform and red/white *krama* associated with that grim organisation.

some uniforms from the NVA. These were often purchased with Chinese funds; because it was more economical, the Chinese preferred to supply the Khmer Rouge with cash for buying uniforms and equipment rather than shipping supplies down the Ho Chi Minh Trail.

The most common form of headgear was the soft, round, olive drab or khaki 'Mao cap'. Captured FANK patrol caps were also worn, and could be seen on Khmer Rouge fighters on their triumphant march into Phnom Penh. Also commonly worn by the Khmer Rouge was the *krama*, a peasant scarf worn around the neck or head, most often seen in a red chequered pattern. Footwear was either the rubber sandal or, more often, nothing at all. No branch, unit, or rank insignia existed among the Khmer insurgents.

Khmer Rouge accoutrements were as spartan as their uniforms. Most were of ChiCom origin,

The Executive Officer of the 1st Parachute Brigade, January 1975, wearing a shirt in French camouflage pattern, French jump wings, and French-style shoulder slide ranking of a lieutenant-colonel.

FANK Order of Battle, August 1970

Unit	Location
1 Infantry Bn.[1]	Phnom Penh
2 Infantry Bde.[2]	Kompong Cham
3 Infantry Bde.	Kompong Som
4 Infantry Bde.	Prey Veng
6 Infantry Bde.[3]	Phnom Penh
7 Infantry Bde.[4]	Phnom Penh
10 Infantry Bde.	Kompong Thom
11 Infantry Bde.	Kompong Thom
12 Infantry Bde.[5]	Siem Reap
13 Infantry Bde.	Phnom Penh
14 Infantry Bde.	Sre Khlong
15 Infantry Bde.[6]	Phnom Penh
16 Infantry Bde.	Phnom Penh
17 Infantry Bde.	Long Vek
18 Infantry Bde.	Romeas
Special Bde.[7]	Siem Reap
1 Parachute Bde.	Phnom Penh
2 Parachute Bde.[8]	Long Vek
Signal Bde.	Phnom Penh
Transportation Half-Bde.	Phnom Penh
Armoured Half-Bde.	Phnom Penh
Artillery Half-Bde.	Phnom Penh
Air Defence Half-Bde.	Phnom Penh
Engineer Half-Bde.	Phnom Penh
Lake Bde.	Tonle Sap
Youth Sapper Bde.	Phnom Penh
1 Marine Corps[9]	Kompong Som

Notes: Above table excludes approximately 120 territorial battalions assigned to the four military regions and the Special Military Region.

(1) Commanded by Maj. Ith Suong, later commander of 1 Infantry Division.

(2) Commanded by Lt.Col. Dien Del, later commander of 2 Infantry Division.

(3) Commanded by Lt.Col. Deng Layom, later commander of armoured forces.

(4) Commanded by Maj. Un Kauv, later commander of 7 Infantry Division.

(5) Commanded by Maj. Teap Ben, later commander of ANS resistance forces.

(6) Commanded by Maj. Lon Non, brother of Lon Nol.

(7) Composed of former Khmer Serei resistance forces.

(8) Never brought to strength; disbanded in 1973.

(9) Composed of four battalions; two located on the coast, two stationed outside Phnom Penh.

purchased from the NVA with Chinese funds. A very common item was the ChiCom AK-47 chest pouch. Khmer Rouge commanders also favoured map cases and holsters as symbols of authority. Later in the war, large amounts of captured FANK equipment allowed the Khmer Rouge to outfit themselves with US web gear and munitions pouches. A small amount of Khmer Rouge equipment was also locally made, such as a crude hammock issued to regular forces.

The North Vietnamese Army

The NVA were the primary opponents of the Khmer Republic for the first two years of the war. They combined a conventional approach—using Main Force elements to crush the FANK in set-piece battles—with deep penetration commando attacks, like the devastating sapper raid on Pochentong Airbase in January 1971. By late 1971,

believing the FANK to be broken, the NVA withdrew most of their Main Force elements from the heart of Cambodia and turned the fighting over to the FUNK. Some specialised units, such as sappers and rocket teams, remained; e.g. on 7 October 1972 a Vietnamese sapper force attempted to destroy the FANK APC park inside Phnom Penh. Other NVA maritime units began infiltrating ammunition along the Cambodian coast in April 1972. The NVA also remained prepared to defend their base areas along the lower Mekong corridor, as demonstrated by the August 1972 armoured counter-offensive which they launched against a FANK-ARVN thrust.

Following the 1973 Paris Peace Accords the NVA still maintained some 36,000 troops inside Cambodia. Often encountered was the 367th NVA Sapper Regiment, believed responsible for the April 1973 rocket attacks on Pochentong Airbase. NVA

NVA/VC Order of Battle in Cambodia, February 1973

Unit	Location	Unit	Location
B-3 Front[1]	Ratanakiri Province	512 Autonomous Bn.	Kandal Province
COSVN[2]	Elements in Kratie Province	570 Regional Bn.	Svay Rieng Province
C-40 Division	Kompong Thom Province	F-44 Regional Bn.	Kampot Province
C-50 Division?	Prey Veng Province	F-48 Regional Bn.	Takeo Province
1 NVA Division[3]	Takeo Province	I-10 Sapper Bn.	Vicinity Kompong Chhnang
		I-25 Sapper Bn.	Vicinity Kompong Chhnang
203 Regional Bde.	Siem Reap Province	I-40 Sapper Bn.	North of Phnom Penh
204 Regional Bde.	Vicinity of Tonle Sap	Z-16 Heavy Bn.	Vicinity Prey Veng
367 NVA Sapper		? Transit Bn.	Vicinity Snuol
Group[4]	Kompong Cham Province	? Logistics Bn.	Vicinity Snuol
		? Regional Bn.	Prey Veng Province
25 Regional Bn.	Strung Treng Province		
32 Autonomous Bn.	Vicinity Kandal		
69 Heavy Bn.	Kompong Cham Province		
82 Logistics Bn.	Prey Veng Province		
90 Sapper Bn.?	Mondulkiri Province		
96 Heavy Bn.	Prey Veng Province		
100 Logistics Bn.	Prey Veng Province		
207 Regional Bn.	Vicinity Svay Rieng		
208 Rocket Bn.	Svay Rieng Province		
220 Logistics Bn.	Kratie Province		
250 Logistics Bn.	Mondulkiri Province		
300 Logistics Bn.	Vicinity Kratie		
322 Autonomous Bn.	Prey Veng Province		
370 Regional Bn.	Kratie Province		
400 Logistics Bn.	Kratie Province		
500 Logistics Bn.	Kompong Cham Province		
510 Autonomous Bn.	Prey Veng Province		
511 Autonomous Bn.	Vicinity Kandal		

Notes: Based on FANK and allied intelligence sources compiled through early 1973

(1) B-3 Front was the command structure for NVA/VC elements in the Second Military Region of South Vietnam.

(2) Central Office, South Vietnam was the NVA/VC command structure for all forces in the Third Military Region and most of the Fourth Military Region in South Vietnam.

(3) Includes the 44 Sapper Regiment, 52 Infantry Regiment, and 101D Infantry Regiment. Most of the division withdrawn from north of Phnom Penh in summer 1972.

(4) A brigade-sized unit. Incorporated into the 5 NVA Division in September 1973 and moved to Tay Ninh, South Vietnam.

anti-aircraft units were also thought to be responsible for heavy fire encountered around Kompong Thom and Takeo in the same month.

By December 1974 the NVA presence had been reduced to 26,200 men, of whom only 12,000 were combat troops. A chilling of relations with the Khmer Rouge, occasionally leading to open conflict, had in part prompted the steep decline in direct NVA participation. However, as late as the 1975 offensive on Phnom Penh, Pol Pot was to make note of NVA artillery support that contributed to the final victory.

Because NVA forces were well known to have operated in Cambodian sanctuaries for years, Hanoi made little effort to conceal the identity of NVA soldiers participating in direct fighting against the Khmer Republic. As a result, Vietnamese casualties encountered on the battlefield invariably wore the standard NVA uniforms and accoutrements seen in South Vietnam.

The Plates

A1: Sergeant, FARK, 1969

During the 1960s the FARK spent much of its time and resources repairing roads and building bridges as part of an extensive civic action programme. As a result, it had little combat experience when Prince Sihanouk sanctioned anti-Khmer Rouge and limited anti-Vietnamese operations in the late 1960s. The FARK had also become the recipient of a confusing array of Western and Eastern Bloc equipment after US military aid was terminated in 1964. This NCO wears French M1947 fatigues and US leather boots, common issue to lower FARK ranks by 1969. Bush hats were also widely used, including these large-brimmed French jungle hats. The weapon is an AK-47 assault rifle, supplied in substantial numbers both by the Eastern Bloc and China during the mid-1960s. Locally-produced

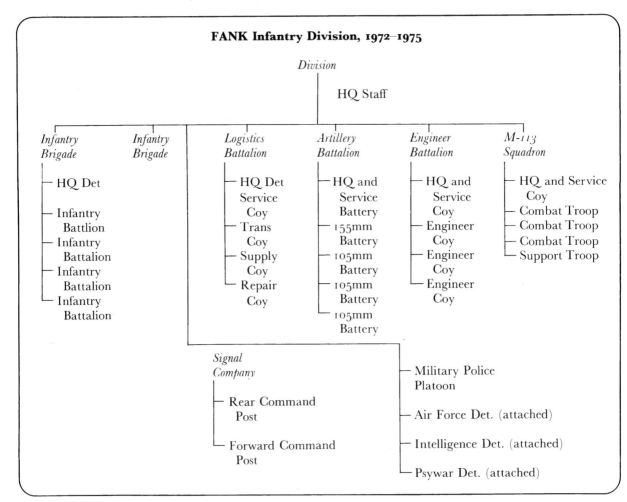

FANK Infantry Division, 1972–1975

canvas pouches are secured by shoulder straps and waist tapes.

A2: Khmer Serei guerrilla, 1969

The Khmer Serei (Free Khmer) were an anti-Communist resistance group led by the Cambodian nationalist Son Ngoc Thanh. Throughout the 1960s they waged a simmering struggle to topple the Sihanouk government. The Khmer Serei were also loosely aligned with the Khmer Kampuchea Krom, a Cambodian faction attempting to gain autonomy for the Khmer Krom people living in South Vietnam's Mekong Delta. Members of both organisations fought on occasion in unconventional warfare units run by the US Army Special Forces.

The Khmer Serei operated from two staging bases: one in the Dongrek Mountains along the Thai border, and one in South Vietnam's IV Corps. This guerrilla operates from South Vietnam, as evidenced by the identifying red scarf (*krama*) he wears around his neck: Dongrek Khmer Serei wore yellow and blue scarfs. On his green beret he wears a metal badge borrowed from the Khmer Kampuchea Krom, depicting a Cambodian flag over an outline of the ARVN IV Corps—a subtle hint at their ultimate goals of autonomy. The Khmer Serei never developed insignia of their own.

Because the Khmer Serei supported autonomy for the ethnic Khmer living in the Mekong Delta, they could not count on assistance from the South Vietnamese government. Commonly worn were camouflage uniforms from the South Vietnamese Police Field Force (a Saigon ruling prohibiting the sale of camouflage to non-military Cambodian personnel excluded the Field Force uniform, making it more readily available to the Khmer

A MEDTC officer visits the 1st Parachute Brigade during operations along the Bassac River, November 1974. He wears subdued Cambodian parachute wings over his right pocket. The paratrooper at left wears the red beret with the standard FANK beret badge.

Serei). Footwear is a black-dyed pair of Bata boots. Accoutrements used by the Khmer Serei rarely amounted to more than simple bandoliers, acquired through sympathetic ARVN channels. The weapon is a CAR-15 carbine; US weapons were used while operating out of South Vietnam to prevent their being mistaken for Communist insurgents. The Khmer Serei staging out of the Dongrek Mountains used the AK-47, a more practical weapon that allowed them to use captured FARK ammunition.

The Buddhist amulets hanging from a gold chain were typical of the Khmer Serei. To protect the guerrilla during an attack, the centre amulet was put in the mouth.

A3: Private, 1ᵉʳ Bataillon de Parachutistes, 1971
The Airborne Half-Brigade, composed of the *1ᵉʳ* and *2ⁱᵉᵐᵉ Bataillons de Parachutistes*, had the most combat

experience of any Cambodian unit before 1970, seeing action in the initial anti-Khmer Rouge campaign of 1967 and the sweeps of Ratanakiri Province in November 1969. After March 1970 the two existing airborne battalions formed the core for an envisaged brigade group totalling eight battalions. Only seven battalions had actually been fielded when a FANK reorganisation in February 1973 cut the paras back to a single brigade of four battalions. While overrated during the first years of the war, the paras had become by late 1974 one of the most effective FANK brigades. They were used extensively in the infantry role. Except for a single battalion-sized parachute drop along the Thai border in 1964—intended to intimidate the Thai government—the Cambodian paratroopers are not thought to have made a combat jump.

In January 1971 President Lon Nol presided over the presentation of the Standard of Victory to three brigades, including 1 Para Bde. This private, taken from a photo of that date, wears the spotted camouflage uniform issued only to Cambodian

MEDTC officer inspecting a FANK mortar position at Svay Rieng garrison, early 1975. Cambodian soldiers wear M1 helmets with camouflage covers and M1956 webbing.

airborne NCOs. He wears an M1945 pistol belt, delivered before the US MAAG was withdrawn in January 1964; hanging from the belt are US-produced canteen and ChiCom anti-tank grenades in a locally-produced pouch. On his shoulder is the early insignia for the *1ᵉʳ Bataillon de Parachutistes*, replaced in 1971 by a new system of airborne insignia featuring an eagle and parachute on a Khmer flag (see Plate F3). The weapon is a Chinese Type 56 light machine gun, a copy of the Soviet RPD.

B1: Cedar Walk, commando, 1971

In 1970 the MACV Studies and Observation group recruited and trained several small teams of Cambodians as airborne commandos in Project 'Cedar Walk'. The teams were deployed in Communist-held regions of north-eastern Cambodia. When the Khmer Republic started to form a Special Forces unit, 20 'Cedar Walk' commandos were airlifted to Cambodia in October 1971 to act as a cadre; a second contingent arrived during the following month. On paper the 'Cedar Walk' operatives were assigned to the Young Khmer Special Forces; because of political pressure, however, they fell under the actual control of the

An MNK Monitor mounting a flamethrower patrols the Mekong; note the anti-rocket grating protecting the super-structure, a highly necessary precaution.

Director of Cambodian Intelligence. As such, they were never properly employed in a conventional warfare capacity.

'Cedar Walk' commandos were equipped like most SOG-supported indigenous units. This commando's camouflage uniform consists of South Vietnamese tiger-stripes and a matching jungle hat; captured NVA uniforms were also worn. A three-pocket indigenous rucksack is worn, with an M1956 pistol belt. The rifle is an M16. Cedar Walk also had access to ComBloc weaponry while on missions into Cambodia.

B2: Lieutenant, UITG, 1971–1972

Like most UITG personnel, this lieutenant is a member of the US Army Special Forces; he wears a UITG flash, based on the Khmer Republican flag, on his green beret. In deference to his Cambodian students his rank is worn French-style on a chest tab and on FANK shoulder loops. A UITG 'Republique Khmere' title is worn on the upper right sleeve; frequently, a UITG battalion training camp insignia was worn underneath. A US Army Special

Forces shoulder insignia and Airborne title are worn on the left shoulder. A CIB and US jump wings are over the left pocket, subdued ARVN Special Forces wings over the right.

B3: FANK private, Long Hai Training Camp, 1972
A young Cambodian recruit at a UITG training base in South Vietnam. He has been issued with US OG 107 fatigues and M1956 LBE, which he will bring back to Cambodia on completion of training. His LBE supports universal pouches, a first aid pouch, a flashlight, a bayonet and a canteen. Because FANK units arrived in South Vietnam as organised battalions, they often came with brigade or battalion insignia already designed and worn on the left shoulder. His weapon is the M16. The UITG programme also equipped FANK battalions with M79 grenade launchers, Browning automatic rifles, .30 cal. machine guns and .50 cal. machine guns.

C1: Khmer Rouge commander, 1975
A Khmer Rouge field commander advances on

The MV *Timberjack* arrives in Phnom Penh in January 1975—the last vessel to make the journey. Note the sand-bagged bridge, and RPG damage to the superstructure.

Phnom Penh during the final offensive against the FANK. By the final year of the war even the most puritanical Khmer Rouge had been forced to adopt items of clothing procured through the NVA. The khaki Mao cap and olive drab shirt were supplied through the North Vietnamese. The sandals and peasant pants, however, display an important sense of commitment to the spartan virtues of Khmer Rouge extremism. A ChiCom chest pouch carries four spare magazines for his AK-47 rifle. As with the Pathet Lao and Viet Cong, Khmer Rouge commanders wore no rank insignia but could be distinguished by the presence of coveted military equipment. This commander carries both a ChiCom leather map case and a canteen.

C2: Khmer Rouge guerrilla, 1974
The uniform items and accoutrements displayed by the guerrilla hint at the various supply channels that were feeding rapidly-growing Cambodian

Communist forces late in the war. His khaki Mao cap and black uniform have been procured through NVA channels. Over his shoulder is the locally-made grenade bandolier carrying rounds for his captured M79 launcher. Chinese-made stick grenades are carried in a locally-made pouch. The sandals have been cut from a truck tyre. Around his neck is the *krama*, a traditional Cambodian scarf, alternatively worn around the forehead by the Khmer Rouge.

C3: Khmer Rouge guerrilla, 1973

Dressed in locally-produced peasant pyjamas and a khaki Mao cap, he erects a makeshift 107mm rocket launcher out of cut branches. A more sophisticated two-shot launcher on a simple metal tripod was also used. Rocket accuracy was poor, but adequate for hitting sprawling cities like Phnom Penh. Weighing 19kg and with a range in excess of 8,000m, the 107mm rocket became the chosen projectile of the Khmer Rouge. Less frequently now, the Khmer Rouge still employ ChiCom 107mm rockets against the Vietnamese occupational forces in Cambodia.

D1: Khmer Air Force UH-1 gunship, 1973–1975

In May 1973 six UH-1 helicopter gunships were turned over to the KAF. Armament was an M60 machine gun on a side-swivel mount. In all ten gunships were delivered, being used extensively in the Mekong convoy support rôle. Cambodian helicopter gunships all had an eagle holding a dagger painted on the nose. A red-coloured eagle indicated helicopters stationed at Phnom Penh; those painted in orange were from Battambang.

The same design was worn as the unit insignia by crews. The KAF national insignia, inspired by US Air Force markings, is painted on the tail boom.

D2: FANK M113 APC, 1971–1976

In 1970 the FARK armoured Demi-Brigade was composed of vintage M24 tanks, AM8 Armoured cars and M2 half-tracks modified into wheeled vehicles. The FANK increased armoured strength to a brigade during the following year, receiving a total of 202 M113 armoured personnel carriers, including 17 examples equipped with a 107mm mortar. In late 1972, M113 APC squadrons were formed in each of the four FANK divisions. Additional APCs were kept in the armoured cavalry headquarters in Phnom Penh, located in the former Olympic stadium.

This FANK M113 is equipped with a .50 cal. machine gun turret and a 106mm recoilless rifle, capable of firing a 9.8kg anti-personnel round over an effective range of 1,100 metres. The Cambodian numeral '13' and a FANK armoured brigade insignia, copied from the design used by the ARVN, are painted on the side.

E1: Khmer Air Force loadmaster, 1971

In May 1971 six KAF transport personnel were brought to Udorn Air Base, Thailand, for training in the AC-47 gunship. They returned to Phnom Penh in June with two gunships, employing them immediately in support of a government garrison

KAF T-28 Trojan fighter-bombers taxi out at Pochentong Airbase outside Phnom Penh during the final months of the war.

43

MEDTC 'novelty insignia' made up for personnel after the fall of the Khmer Republic. The '102' refers to the number of days the MEDTC stayed in Cambodia after the 1975 New Year offensive began.

60km south-west of the capital. By 1973 the KAF was operating 12 gunships, using them primarily for Mekong convoy support and night operations.

This sergeant was the loadmaster in the original Udorn contingent in May 1971. He wears a Thai leaf-camouflage flight suit procured by the first crew on graduation. The black scarf around his neck is decorated with the 'Spooky' gunship ghost insignia ('Spooky' was the radio callsign for USAF, Laotian and South Vietnamese AC-47 gunships). The scarf also bears the word 'Lougaru', a corruption of the French word for werewolf, which was the KAF AC-47 callsign. The insignia over his left breast was designed and produced by the first KAF AC-47 crew; subsequent Cambodian AC-47 personnel wore a squadron insignia showing the *garuda*, a mythical seven-headed serpent. The blue overseas cap was standard in the KAF. Footwear is the US jungle boot.

E2: Khmer Air Force captain, 1972
In 1972 ten KAF T-28s were damaged or destroyed during combat operations, most due to mechanical failure or pilot error. At least one airman was believed captured by the Khmer insurgents.

Intimidated by these statistics, this KAF fighter-bomber pilot wears a 'blood-chit' based on the design of the Republican flag, reading, 'If you capture me, please treat me as a POW according to international agreements'. Since neither the NVA nor the Khmer Rouge were known to keep many Cambodian prisoners alive, such pleas were almost certainly in vain. It is also noteworthy that the Vietnamese translation in the middle contains several spelling errors. Translation in Khmer and Chinese are also included. A Khmer flag and KAF title are worn on the left shoulder of the pilot's US flight suit. He wears a blue peaked cap with silver KAF badge.

E3: FANK brigadier-general, 1973
The commander of the Khmer Special Forces, Brig. Gen. Thach Reng, is seen wearing the olive green FANK dress uniform. The peaked cap has the gold FANK device depicting the Angkor Wat temple complex. Buttons bear the combined service emblem of the FANK General Headquarters. Brigadier-general's rank is displayed on black French-style shoulder boards. Special Forces insignia with a *Forces Speciales* tab is seen on the upper left sleeve. Metal Cambodian basic wings are worn on the upper right chest, and US basic wings, received after his training at Long Thanh, South Vietnam, on the left.

F1: Sergeant, Khmer Special Forces, 1973
In early 1973 several FANK detachments were sent to Lopburi Special Warfare Centre, Thailand, for advanced ranger and communications training; the latter was needed to provide the Khmer Special Forces with radio operators for its small-unit operations behind enemy lines. Upon their return to Cambodia they saw heavy fighting at Kompong Cham in September 1973, helping the FANK successfully defend the city by calling in accurate aerial resupply drops.

This sergeant is wearing a new set of camouflage fatigues designed and issued specifically for the Khmer Special Forces trainees attending courses at Lopburi; while its colours appear bright, they quickly faded to a duller, more effective pattern. Cambodian para wings are worn over the right pocket. The insignia of his current unit, the Special Forces, is on the left shoulder; the insignia of the

FANK Signal Corps, his original unit, is on the right shoulder. The green beret bears a handwoven SF flash.

F2: Corporal, Bataillon de Fusiliers-Marins, 1973
The MNK Marine Corps remained a small static defence force during the first three years of the war. In 1973 the MNK was authorised to double its strength, including an expansion of the Marines to 11 battalions. BFM deployment paralleled the FANK, with the Marines fighting an interdiction force along most of the country's major waterways. By December 1973 one BFM was patrolling the coastline, four were providing harbour security and four were on operations along the Mekong corridor. Two additional battalions, composed of disbanded FANK territorial forces, were formed in 1974.

F3: Captain, 1st Parachute Brigade, 1973
Two battalions of 1 Para Bde. were among the initial reinforcements sent to the besieged provincial capital of Kompong Cham on 21 August 1973. Fighting their way across the city, the paras turned back repeated Communist assaults until further FANK reinforcements could be landed along the Mekong waterfront behind Communist lines. The two forces linked up and drove the Communists out of Kompong Cham by 13 September. Two remaining para battalions were heliborne on to the airfield north of the city during the opening days of the siege, and withstood continuous enemy pressure until relieved by KAF security troops in mid-September.

This captain wears French-style camouflage uniform, usually limited to use by paratroop officers. His red beret bears no cap badge; FANK airborne units never created a cap badge, although a cloth version of the FANK national insignia (see Plate E3) or metal wings were used as such. On his left shoulder is the insignia for 1 Para Brigade. Above this are ballpoint pens—always the symbol of authority in Indo-Chinese armed forces. On both collars are rank insignia, generally adopted after 1972.

G1: Captain, MEDTC, 1971–1975
To observe equipment utilisation and FANK unit performance, MEDTC personnel were assigned to work with specific FANK, MNK and KAF formations. The branch orientation of a MEDTC team member was often matched to a Cambodian counterpart: this MEDTC captain, a member of the US Army Special Forces, is assigned to the Khmer Special Forces and 1 Airborne Brigade. His leaf camouflage uniform is of South Vietnamese

1985: Khmer Rouge guerrillas, now wearing Chinese-made olive drab uniforms, float a Chinese Type 53 heavy machine gun across the Tonle Sap.

origin, having been purchased on a previous tour. He wears subdued Khmer instructor wings, awarded at the Airborne Training Centre at Pochentong Airbase, over the right shirt pocket; subdued US Army Special Forces insignia, marking his previous unit in South Vietnam on the right shoulder; and a MEDTC title on the left shoulder. Cambodian-style rank insignia are embroidered on a Khmer Republic flash.

MEDTC personnel remained in the field for only short periods, during which times they were allowed to be lightly armed. This captain carries a privately-acquired UZI sub-machine gun and wears an M56 belt with a holstered Hi-Power Browning.

G2: FANK reconnaissance team member, 1974
When the UITG was training FANK battalions in 1971 and 1972, reconnaissance platoons were occasionally sent for additional training. Further FANK reconnaissance units were trained in early 1972 at Phitsanulok, Thailand. Five hundred FANK trainees at Phitsanulok were put through a Commando Raider course; upon their return to Cambodia, they were divided into teams and assigned as pathfinders for infantry formations. In November 1972 a Recondo School was opened in Battambang Province to further expand the number of reconnaissance units available to the FANK. By 1974 most FANK brigades had a reconnaissance platoon, and each division had a recondo company.

Graduates from the FANK Recondo School were issued Cambodian tiger-stripe uniforms with matching bush hat. LBE is the standard FANK M1956 pattern. He carries an M203 rifle/grenade launcher combination—one of only 55 delivered to the FANK. On his shoulder is the insignia of the Recondo Company of the 2nd FANK Division. Instructors at the Recondo School wore a shoulder patch bearing an inverted black triangle with an eagle, copies from the emblem of the Royal Thai Army LRRP School.

G3: Lieutenant, Para-Commando Battalion, 1975
Sixty FANK students attended training at the respected Airborne Commando School at Batu Djadjar, Indonesia in mid-1972. After a six-month course two dozen Muslim members of the contingent were posted to the FANK 5th Infantry Brigade, a predominantly Muslim formation; the remainder formed a ceremonial unit in Phnom Penh until 1974. They were then used as the cadre for a new Para-Commando battalion loosely assigned to the Khmer Special Forces, and sent to fight on the northern perimeter of Phnom Penh.

The commandos trained at Batu Djadjar were completely outfitted by the Indonesians before returning to Cambodia; this para-commando retains his Indonesian camouflage uniform and jump-wings. An M1 steel helmet is worn; a red beret, standard among all Cambodian airborne battalions, was also issued to the para commandos. The M16 rifle, M1956 LBE and jungle boots are FANK issue.

H1: Honour Guard, PRKAF, 1980
Sixteen days after Vietnam invaded Cambodia in December 1978 a proxy government called the People's Republic of Kampuchea was installed in Phnom Penh. The PRK Armed Forces have been slowly built up by the Vietnamese, but are rated as only marginally reliable. PRKAF defections to the resistence forces are frequent, and, until 1988, no PRK units operated in contested border regions without their Vietnamese equivalent alongside. In 1988 the PRKAF was estimated at 35,000 troops, including five infantry divisions used primarily for static defence.

Pictured during a 1980 parade in Phnom Penh, this member of the PRK Honour Guard wears a white dress uniform and peaked cap with metal PRKAF badge. A medal honouring the Khmer forces which helped defeat the Khmer Rouge in 1978 is worn on the right chest. The rifle is a Soviet SKS carbine, with a PRK flag sticking from the barrel. In the field, PRK forces wear Vietnamese-style olive drab or khaki fatigues. Headgear is usually an olive drab Mao cap or khaki field cap. Accoutrements are of Vietnamese origin.

H2: Khmer Rouge guerrilla, 1986
After the Vietnamese invasion in late 1978, the Khmer Rouge withdrew toward the Thai border in an orderly fashion and created a guerrilla staging area based in the Cardamon Mountains. In 1987 they maintained an estimated 35,000 guerrillas organised into regiments and light divisions. Funding comes primarily from the People's Republic of China.

The Khmer Rouge now claim to have tempered their extremist ideology, which resulted in the deaths of perhaps two million Cambodians while they were in power from 1975 to 1978. As 'proof' of their new moderate outlook, Khmer Rouge regulars have now exchanged their spartan black pyjamas for green fatigues shipped directly from China. No branch or rank insignia are worn. Aside from a metal cap badge designed for a Khmer Rouge Honour Guard in 1985, no other Khmer Rouge unit insignia exist. The weapon is an RPG-7. His sandals are made at Site 8, the Khmer Rouge-run refugee camp on the Thai-Cambodian border.

H3: KPNLF guerrilla, 1987

In October 1979, 1,500 anti-Communist resistance fighters along the Cambodian border unified under the banner of the Khmer People's National Liberation Front. Three years later the movement joined the UN-recognised Coalition government of Democratic Kampuchea, an anti-Vietnamese resistance umbrella organisation which includes the Khmer Rouge and forces loyal to Prince Sihanouk (the National Sihanoukist Army, or ANS). The KPNLF peaked in strength in 1983, when its 12,000

KPNLF guerrillas in Siem Reap Province, 1984. They are armed with AK-47s, RPGs and an M79. Clothing is a random mixture of various camouflage and olive drab items with civilian garments.

armed combatants successfully defended their border enclaves from a Vietnamese dry season attack. The following year the Vietnamese returned in greater strength, driving all three of the resistance factions across the Thai border. Since that time the KPNLF has tried to regain momentum by fielding small commando units in the border provinces.

While the KPNLF receives non-lethal assistance from the USA, China and the Association of South East Asian Nations (ASEAN), military assistance comes primarily from China and captured sources. This guerrilla wears Thai tiger-stripes and jungle boots. Other uniforms include civilian peasant clothes, green fatigues and Thai leaf-camouflage. His weapon is the ChiCom Type 56 rifle with folding stock, the most common firearm in the resistance coalition. The AK-47 chest pouch is also of Chinese origin. On his left shoulder is the KPNLF emblem. Individual KPNLF battalion insignia are worn on the left shoulder or on baseball-type caps. A black scarf has been adopted as headgear.

Index

Figures in **bold** refer to illustrations. Plates are shown with page and caption locators in brackets.